THE WAR JOURNAL

(1999-2010)

Volume II

THE WAR JOURNAL

(1999-2010)

Volume II

The Seat Of War: The Christian Church In America

The War Stories And Their Meanings

Paula Matthews

$$\text{S} \atop \text{L}$$

Spirit & Life Publications

The War Journal (1999-2010) Volumes I & II

©2010 Paula Matthews

The Narrative And Edited Version Of

The War Journal (1999-2002)

©2002 Paula Matthews

Published by
Spirit & Life Publications
Los Angeles

Printed In The United States Of America

ISBN 978-0-9851172-1-4

"This Coming Move Of God

Is His Grand Finale Before Jesus Comes:

Fire In The Sky And Earth: Fireworks.

It's The Time Of God's Justice:

Good And Bad Rewarded For Their Persistence."

The War Journal (1999-2010) Volume I

Table of Contents

"Let The Wicked Forsake His Way

And The Unrighteous Man His Thoughts:

And

Let Him Return Unto The Lord,

And

He Will Have Mercy Upon Him...

...For He Will Abundantly Pardon."

Isaiah 55:7 KJV

PREFACE

In *The War Journal (1999-2010) Volume I*, we explored the journal entries and explained the visions, dreams and prophecies declaring war in America. Although we discussed the causes and reasons for war, there were prophetic stories and teachings from Almighty God too numerous to include in the first book, therefore volume two was started in 2008 to take an in-depth look at the stories the Holy Spirit gave to further explain the causes of war.

It should be noted that according to God, the spiritual <u>*Seat Of War*</u> in America is the Christian Church. He blames the issues and conflicts in America on the hypocrisy and the backslidden condition of the Church. It must be understood that the term *church* or *American Church* is used to describe the religious and denominationally divided congregations of America. Unfortunately, this group accounts for the majority of traditional Christian and Evangelical organizations in the country. These organizations successfully operate by segregating God's people from each other and from the Truth of God, and yet they commonly use the Bible and religious doctrine as a weapon against the people. It is easy to identify such organizations because of their stern teachings and lack of compassion and love. Jesus said that the world would know Christians by their love, and yet the leaders of these organizations have created loveless churches that do not follow the teachings of Jesus Christ; instead they follow rules and religious mandates of men. By definition these are cults, sects and preachers of heresies. On the surface they look Christian, but it is no more than a façade for a purely profit and power motivated operation. Then there are God's Kingdom leaders; those who are true to the teachings of Jesus Christ and promote God's love and compassion for the lost, without prejudice. The organizations these leaders create are modeled after the life and ministry of Jesus Christ. These are kingdom minded individuals who are motivated by obedience to God. God's kingdom leaders often suffer severe persecution from the traditional *church* leaders just like Jesus experienced at the hand of the Pharisees.

In Jesus' day, the Pharisees were the hypocritical religious Jewish leaders who practiced traditional rules of men instead of God's word. They used God's word to chastise and rule over God's people in fear. The Pharisees hated Jesus because of his miracles and message of God's love. Religious leaders of our day rule their congregations with law and fear as well. They are also quite vocal in the political area. The love of God is not in them, so they are not tolerant with those who opinions differ from theirs. These leaders cause great division among denominations over religious doctrine and various interpretations of Bible scripture.

This force of evil doers in the American church has resulted in many believers leaving the faith and abandoning God. Jesus would call them a brood of vipers and children of the devil, and yet they appear to be the most holy and pious of believers. Jesus warned his disciples that these religious leaders would imprison them and put them to death; and that is exactly what some of them have done to God's chosen leaders in our day. They do it all in the name of God, and yet they have never met God.

Unfortunately most Americans have never heard the truth about Jesus Christ or about his kingdom because of prejudiced evil leaders. Religious men have been heard hurling evil rhetoric and claiming to be the voice of God in America. In this book, God will speak for himself and deny his association with this *church*. He starts by clearly blaming the problems of America on the *church*. If more Christian leaders were diligently watching and praying for the leaders of this nation and for the plight of its people, many of America's problems could have been avoided. Instead of standing in the gap for our fellowman and demonstrating the love of God as the Bible instructs, the Church in America has become a political force that demonstrates bigotry while blocking the entrance to God's Kingdom for all those who truly want to seek him.

Truth be known, most of the American church has never gone through that open door to God. Every Sunday they fill church pews looking devout, but in fact, all they hold is a membership card for a local congregation. If they had truly met God, they would reflect the glory of God and not the hatred of Satan. God gave his love and transforming power to the church, so that it could reign in righteous and justice. Instead, hypocrisy has rendered the American Church a weak and non-effective entity; and a weak church creates an environment that fosters a spiritually and financially weakened nation.

In this book we will learn that the condition of the *church* has created a cataclysmic conflict with God akin to when Jonah refused to go to Nineveh. Jonah didn't feel that Nineveh was worthy to be saved; so he got on a boat and headed to another city. Likewise, God has spoken to the church concerning the plight of the United States. Many have been given specific instructions for getting the country back on track. Instead, many pastors and leaders are packing up and heading for Israel. According to the writers of the documentary entitled, *Waiting For Armageddon*, "American Evangelicals donate over $75 million a year to support Israel."[i] The Spirit of God says that this kind of support is being done by the church while ignoring the Biblical mandate to care for the poor, widows and fatherless within our borders first. The Spirit of God calls this disdain for the poor, *Anti-American* behavior. But God, in his endless mercy and love for the church and our country, will not leave us in our mess. Just like he caused a major storm to force Jonah overboard, the Lord has prepared a storm to overthrow the American church as well; and yet, there will be a great fish ready to devour disobedient church leaders. Not only will this wake the church from its slumber, but God will bring forth a mighty army of believers anointed and equipped to calm the storm and to minister to the needs of the victims and survivors of this great disaster; and God will get the glory.

15

The Spirit of God revealed this coming storm in a series of prophecies beginning with one which was received in December 2010 entitled, *"The Foundations are Shaken."*

The foundations are shaken. Be forewarned. All has been shaken!! Take refuge in My Kingdom! All has been shaken, says the Spirit of Grace.' Now is the time says God, to answer the cries of the righteous, the martyrs who are suffering at the hands of the enemies of God. All is not in vain says God for these cries are the travails of the birthing pains as I bring forth my Sons into the earth; the power of such will cause the heavens and the earth to be shaken. The end of which will be the fullness of my glory manifested in this earth . . . full of grace and power. So be patient and endure suffering for my sake . . . the end of which will be birthed inside of your spirit, the fullness of my power.

The entire world is in crisis and will continue experiencing "shaking" and upheavals until Jesus' return. Whether there be wars, rumors of war, famines, and earthquakes or nations rising up against nations; God has a plan for his kingdom to prosper in spite of these things. Our only means of earthly survival is found in God's Kingdom and its operation. For the wellbeing of all people, believers in Jesus Christ must remain faithful to God and his plan. Proverbs 25:19 says that having confidence in an unfaithful man during a time of trouble is like having a broken tooth and a foot out of joint. We are the Body of Christ; a broken tooth causes much pain, but if the foot is out of joint, the whole body is out of balance and cannot move swiftly in times of trouble. Jesus said that if a member of your body causes you to sin cut it off. It is better to go in to life maimed than to have the whole body cast into Hell. God is about to cut off some members of his body so that the whole church will arise powerful and triumphant in this hour. It is time for the sons of God to take their place and perform *the greater works* Jesus promised we would do.

The world is about to experience tremendous times of darkness; but those in the Kingdom of God will see magnificent works of God in the earth. A remnant of faithful believers will lay hold of heaven's armory and slay the evil giants of fear and oppression. The righteous will take authority and the people will rejoice!

FROM THE AUTHOR

"... I Send Thee To ... A Rebellious Nation

That Hath Rebelled Against Me: They And Their Fathers

*Have Transgressed Against Me, Even Unto This Very Day.
For They Are Impudent Children And Stiff Hearted.*

*I Do Send Thee Unto Them; And Thou Shalt Say Unto
Them, "Thus Saith The Lord God."*

*And They, Whether They Will Hear Or Whether They
Will Forbear, (For They Are A Rebellious House)*

Yet, Shall Know They That

There Hath Been A Prophet Among Them."

Ezekiel 2:3-5

Commissioned Officer Of The Kingdom

In 1997, the Spirit of God called me to the office of the prophet, by speaking the words from Ezekiel 2:3-8. He said he was sending me out like he did the first Apostles; and that I was being sent to the most rebellious of his people with messages of repentance. To this day, God continuously sends me to his leaders. He made it perfectly clear that if I refused to speak God's word to a particular person, then that person's blood would be on my hands.

This statement of reprimand from God has been a constant reminder that I am commissioned under God's Kingdom military command. I am not my own, neither can I act or speak of my own. I am to obey His orders. I learned obedience early on in Holy Ghost Boot Camp. One of my first assignments was to send a prophecy by fax and by mail to a pastor whom I soon learned hated prophets and hated women in ministry. When God gave me the prophecy, it contained a couple of words that were extremely harsh. So, I took the liberty of marking over the words on a written draft of the prophecy while I was on a break from another assignment. Later, when I went back to my car to get the draft, the Presence of God was hovering over my car. The moment I touched the door handle, it felt as though a bolt of electricity went through my body. I opened the door, fell into the seat and closed the car door. Immediately the Voice of God spoke so loud that my entire being was shaken up. *'__How dare you change my words__!'* said God and he began speaking words that to this day echo in my spirit. He let me know that by changing his words, I was being insubordinate to his specific orders. He questioned me as to what other authority I held that could out rank his judgment in this matter. Of course, I had none. To make matters worse he let me know that my judgment call was made without having any clue as to his plan and purpose for this pastor's life. Humbly, I repented and rewrote God's original message exactly how he told me to write it; and I sent it to the pastor.

Six months later, a woman from this same church called me concerned about a prophecy God had her write for her pastor. This was the same man God had me send a message to six months prior; and when she read the prophecy, it was word-for-word the exact thing I had written. I listened quietly as this woman asked what she should do. I told her to deliver the message in the exact wording and manner in which God had instructed her. I never told her that I had written to her pastor as well. And the Spirit of God let me know that the pastor had received the same message before I had written him as well. From that assignment on, I have learned that I can never presume to know the heart or mind of God unless he reveals it specifically to me. My job is just to obey; and it has not always been easy.

God has sent me on some of the most difficult assignments, and yet for those who received the word, there have been notable miracles. Many of such miracles are recorded in *The War Journal (1999-2010) Volume I*. God loves his people so much that he repeatedly put my life in danger in order to give them one last word of hope. It has not been an easy assignment, because like most people, I don't like to suffer. Coming from a deadly divorce and an evil encounter with organized crime, I was hoping for a simple relaxing position in the Kingdom of God, but it was not to be. The Spirit of God explained that my personal tragedies were Basic Training that would enable me to handle what God called, *'THE REAL CRIMINALS;'* the leaders of the American Church who are using mafia tactics to *'kill'* God's people. More shocking as this sounded, my experience has proven that it was easier dealing with the organized criminals in Chicago than it was dealing with church leaders.

With organized criminals in the world, corruption is their business; and they mean business. Is there honor among thieves? I don't know; but, I have seen the Holy Spirit move upon criminal hearts to spare my life. According, to God, my ex-husband told some people that I knew something that I did not know. As a result, they put a contract out on my life. Even though I didn't understand all; I clearly recognized the spirit of death as it hovered over me continuously. The enemy plotted a deadly plan against me, but God had another plan. He moved upon the same men who plotted to kill me, and instead they blessed me. They passed anonymous messages to me in court. One man even showed up in divorce court and spoke with me about what I knew about my ex. I never saw the man's face because my head was down, tears were in my eyes and I could only focus on the fact that my son had been kidnapped by his father and I was trapped into a deadly game in court. But before I left the court room this unknown man took my hand and gave me a verbal blessing and said that this was his desire for my life.

It wasn't until I returned home that a pastor friend called and said a group of them had been praying for me while I was in court. And she said 'You met the boss today; not the man he says he works for; the mob boss.' And while I argued that I had not met anyone, the Holy Spirit interrupted me and reminded me of the man who blessed me in court. Then he said, 'You are free. The contract was cancelled.' As the Holy Spirit revealed this to me, my friend also got a revelation from God and we both rejoiced knowing that only God could have touched the hearts of those who were once determined to kill me, and use them for his glory. This story had a glorious end, but ironically the stories involving church leaders have not been so glorious.

There is a spirit of pride and arrogance that often overcomes leaders of the American church that prevents them from accepting any spirit of correction. There is a misconception that if God called them, then it is indication that they are perfect in the eyes of God. Even God, himself cannot reach people with this attitude, and yet these are exactly the people to whom I was sent. These leaders pretend to be lovers of God, and yet they have no problem plotting to kill their brothers, in the name of the Lord. They are the proverbial wolves in sheep's clothing waiting to devour their prey. I thank God that each time he sent me in to these imposters the Lord provided me a safe way to escape. Each message was delivered and the task completed.

Did I suffer? Indeed I did. There were days when the suffering was so great, and there was no relief in sight. All I could do was curl up in the arms of God, in his secret place and take refuge. But in all, this was truly a labor of love. When things got rough, God reminded me of Jesus' suffering on the cross, and I began to see how Jesus could endure the suffering for the joy of a greater purpose being revealed in another person's life. Suffering during obedience to God's command is what it means to take up your cross and follow him. Surely, I am a better person because of this commission. Through my obedience, God has taught me how to love the way he loves and how to live a life that is full of purpose.

Fighting The Good Fight Of Faith

Once you receive God's word concerning your destiny in this life, it attaches itself to the deepest longing of your soul. My greatest joy in life was when God's seed was implanted within my heart. It became my purpose for living; the breath of heaven filling my thoughts with all the good and future hope of what is to come. This is the air I breathe throughout every day. Although the details of my future are yet unknown, the anticipation of God's highest good for my life, is exhilarating. With my entire being, I embrace that which God desires for my life. This is the Christ in me, the hope of God's glory to be revealed in me: my Eternal Purpose in Christ.

My journal of faith has been long and trying. I now know what it means to fight the good fight of faith. When God reveals your purpose in life, you have to be prepared to battle for your life and for your dream. In spiritual terms, the most dangerous person on the planet earth is the individual who actual seeks God, finds and accepts God's will for their life. An individual whose eyes are wide open to the truth of God's purpose for men in this world, could potentially set men free, just by walking out God's path for their own life. This person is a danger to Satan and his kingdom: the god of this world who has bamboozled the minds and hearts of men throughout the world. He is the father of lies; the master of deception. But when God begins to reveal truth, Satan's lies have no further power over you. Blinded eyes are opened to hidden details that change one's life from darkness to light, and from cursed to blessed, from death to life; and not just any life, but the highest form of life available to men on earth: Zoë,[i] the God kind of life. We call it Eternal Life. It begins on earth when we find God and accept his purpose.

The church in America has taught that Eternal Life is what you receive when you die. No! When you receive Jesus as Lord of your life, you exchange your limited human existence for God's infinite possibilities. From the moment you decide to follow Jesus, you latch onto a life that is eternal; a life that has its source in Heaven.

You will no longer desire to know men and what they desire for your life. You will long for God's desire to be fulfilled within you. I love what Jesus said, *'And this is life eternal, that they would know God and Jesus Christ whom you have sent.'*[lii] Our Eternal Life begins when we receive and pursue after knowledge of God; his thoughts, his ways, his desires for our lives. We are then commanded to be *imitators* of God like obedient children.[liii] It sounds like an ethereal and lofty task, because it cannot be done in our human strength. Thank God for his Holy Spirit that teaches us the ways of God and gives us the strength to obtain all that God desires for us in this life.

Many things seem impossible for man; but with God all things are possible. We must rely on him and allow him to have his way in our lives because our vision of life is limited. God's vision of life has no end. His vision is infinite; eternal. In comparison, we are like ants busy about in our own world and totally oblivious to the existence of God or anyone outside of that little world. We set our goals to be the biggest ant on the ant hill and call it accomplishment. How ignorant! To build the biggest ant hill makes you the most visible target for a giant who wants to stomp you down to the ground. Satan and death are the giants in this world that want to stomp us six feet under the ground; they want to steal our lives. The only protection we have on earth is found in the Kingdom of God. Jesus told his followers to accumulate treasures in Heaven where they cannot be destroyed by anything on this earth. What God gives us from heaven, can never be taken by anyone. We can give it away in our ignorance or out of fear, but what God gives us is eternally ours.

God's gift of Eternal Life is the most valuable treasure in existence. It's not about dying and going to Heaven; it is about creating Heaven upon the earth; God's will being done on earth, as it is in Heaven. Imagine the unlimited wealth, health, protection and supernatural gifts of Heaven becoming available for your daily use here on earth. Eternal Life is for us now. To obtain this gift is man greatest pleasure; but to keep it safely is our greatest challenge in life. Although it is protected by heaven, we have an enemy whose goal is to deceive us into believing that what God has given us and what God says is not true. This is our *fight of faith*: a battle of God's word for your life versus all other words spoken to control your life with lies; including Satan's lies, the evil words of friends and family, even the evil words and thoughts you have about yourself, and every evil circumstance of deception and every obstacle that is place along your path. In our human strength it is an impossible battle, but that is why God gives us his Holy Spirit to be our teacher and guide. He will tell us how to navigate the course of this new way of life. He will also alert us to the lies, deceptions and obstacles. He will also relay God's plan of escape directly to us. This is how our human impossibilities become divine possibilities.

My greatest disappoint along my journey of faith has been the loss of people who were previously attached to my vision, but whom no longer desired to follow God. Whether it was jealousy, anger, resentment or envy, in strife they all tried to make me stumble off the path God designed for me. Satan wanted to use them to kill me and my dream; even though I have shared my dream with anyone, but Satan knew. People want what you have, but they are unwilling to do what it takes to get what you have. Their remaining tactic is to attempt to keep you from fulfilling your God given dream; but they have no power to stop God's plan for your life. Even Satan doesn't have that power.

God often reminded me of the story of when Joseph shared his divine dreams with his family. Joseph was hated because his father Jacob loved him the more than his brothers. When he shared his dreams the brothers hated Joseph even more, and they plotted to kill him. They were so filled with envy and hatred that the brothers could not see that Joseph's dream meant a bright prosperous future for the entire family.[iv] This is important to know while we are fighting the good fight of faith. Our dream is not just about us. God has a way of giving us a dream that supplies a need for families, communities and nations; although God gives the dream to us; it's not all about us.

Now, Joseph's brothers and even their father Jacob could have sought God to find out what else was in store for the family. Anyone can seek God for their own dream, but many will not do so. People cannot see God when their hearts are filled with hate and envy; they see only red; as in the blood they wish to shed. This has been demonstrated in my journey of faith. After *The War Journal (1999-2010) Volume I* was published in September 2011, the Spirit of God informed me that most of those who were called to continue with me on this journey had all jumped ship. Even my pending marriage was not to happen, which derailed the remainder of this project. The Spirit of God told me to be faithful until death and he had me write out my Last Will and Testament. None of these things settled well with me until I recalled something the Lord told me at the inception of this project years ago. The Spirit of God told me that if I refused to obey him, I would be replaced with a more faithful person. Since that promise, I have made this project my sole reason for living. If I could not please God by completing the task he gave me, then there was no real reason for me to stay on earth. The overwhelming desire of my heart was to finish this project and honor the God who thought me worthy enough to allow such significance to my trust.

Then I began pleading with God in prayer that this one promise be applied again. After all, before I left Los Angeles, the Lord told me to tell the team that the project would 'Go forth no matter what.' And besides, when I was abandoned the first time, God gave me a brand new team. I didn't like starting over with a new team, but I had no choice. I had to either petition God for another chance or give up and die. It was a short time after this plea that the Spirit of God told me, *'You are free!'* Hallelujah! I was no longer chained to a defiant man and his curses.

The worst thing you can do in God's kingdom is to start a project in obedience and then abandon ship because the fire gets a little hot. The Bible says that anyone who puts his hand to the plough and then looks back is not fit for the kingdom. Believers are supposed to endure to the end. And here's some good news. When we obey God, we may be thrown into a fiery furnace, but we always come out without a burn and we won't even smell of smoke. Our attitude as believers should be like the three Hebrew boys before they were thrown into the fiery furnace. They let the king know that their God had the power to deliver them, but if God chose not to deliver them from the fire, they still refused to bow down and serve another god. If Jesus submitted unto God to the agony and suffering of the cross so that we could have Eternal Life, who are we to back down from what God asks of us. If we are true disciples of Jesus, we must follow his example and take up our cross and follow him. When we obey God, he will always be faithful to his word. He will not let us down. We have to earnestly contend for the faith that we profess. A contender is one who strives to obtain a reward. Jesus said that we must strive to enter into the narrow gate into God's kingdom because many will seek to enter, but they won't be able.

On my faith journey many have come, but many left because God required us to walk a narrow road. The church has taught us that once saved, there is no further requirement; but in the mind of God, accepting the cross is just the beginning. Next we must, seek the Kingdom of God and the road God requires us to travel. If we are truly listening, the road will be challenging, but the rewards well worth the journey.

Although the details of the remainder of my journey of faith are yet to be revealed, I eagerly look forward to the treasures that God has hidden along the way. With all its difficulties and obstacles, I would not change the course that God has set for my life; for in every victory, I've learn that in my weakness, he is strong, and in my impossibility, he always reveals that he is the God of possibilities. Deuteronomy 29:29 says that the secret or hidden things belong to God, but the things he reveals belong to God's people and their children. I will continue to strive for the kingdom treasures; not just for me, but I intend to leave an awesome spiritual inheritance for my children's children.

INTRODUCTION

"Every Kingdom Divided Against Itself

Is Brought To Desolation

And Every City Or House

Divided Against Itself Shall Not Stand."

Matthew 12:25

A Kingdom Divided

When the Spirit of God told me to write this sequel to *The War Journal (1999-2010) Volume I*, he gave me a vision of the Christian Church in America. In this vision I saw a beautiful, powerful body. It was a muscular and strong body in the image of a man. God said it was the American Church. It stood as a very impressive figure. Then the body turned to the side and began to walk. When the figure began to walk, the body moved but the head remained in its place. The body continued to walk as if it had a head, but there was no head attached. How could this be? At the beginning of the vision the head and body appeared to be attached, but when the body moved, the Lord gave me a closer view of the neck; there were no tears or loose skin fragments at the neck. This was an indication that there was no severing of the head from the body. It became obvious that the head and body were never connected at all.

My heart was astonished. How could America create such a powerful church and yet be deceived into thinking it was following God? Then it occurred to me that the human body is controlled by electrical impulses from the brain. If the Body of Christ in America had no head, how was it even able to move? Where was this body getting its impulses? If Jesus is not leading the church, who was? The Spirit of God gave me a daunting explanation that I will never forget; the American Church had formed an organized rebellion against the Kingdom of God. The Lord said that the Body of Christ in America is in agreement with all its members that it doesn't need a head in order to survive. He said that they have built a church in the similitude of the Tower of Babel. The people of Babel were of one mind and one language when they decided to build a tower so that they could reach to heaven and make a name for themselves. The builder of Babel was Nimrod, the great grandson of Noah. God made a covenant with Noah and his family that they would govern their lives to honor God. So while the builders of the Tower of Babel were in agreement with each other, they were in rebellion against God by violating the covenant.[v]

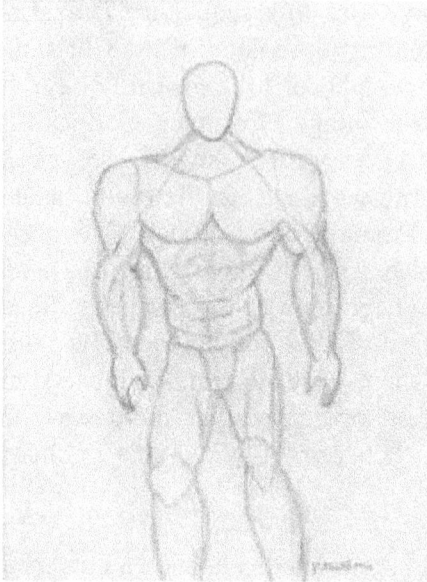

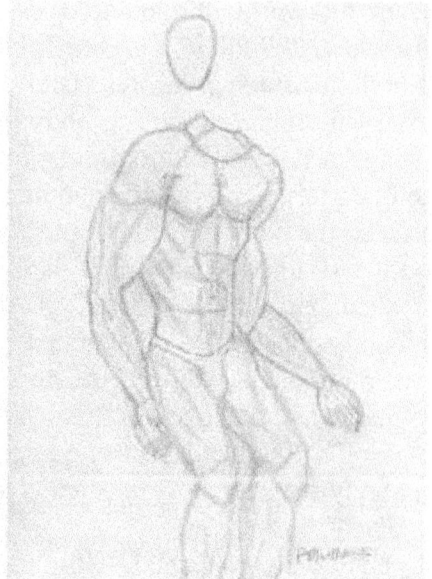

The Body of Christ in America (the Church)   The Body of Christ without the Head

Likewise, leaders of the American Christian church have erected a structure they think will help them reach heaven without God; a form of church to exalt themselves; and like the Tower of Babel, they will be scattered by God. Exaltation comes from God. He is the judge. He puts down one and sets up another.[vi] Thankfully, God in his mercy will not leave America a spiritual orphan. He is determined that all know about his love, plan and purpose for every man on earth, in spite of those who have misrepresented him in the past. Therefore, God will raise up His Church: those who are one with the mind, plan and purpose of God. Rather than speaking their own words, they will be like Jesus when he said that he says and does only what God the father says and does in Heaven.[vii] Nothing shall be impossible for them, for they will do all God the father has imagined and purposed for men on earth.

The Biblical concept of *submission* usually sends shock waves throughout American churches, yet it was while under submission that Jesus displayed the greatest power. Jesus was accused of casting out demons with the power of Beelzebub, the chief of the devils. He said that Satan would never come against one of his own demons. He said that a kingdom divided against itself would be ruined and a house divided against itself will fall. Then Jesus said that if he cast out demons with the finger (instruction and power) of God, then the Kingdom of God was in their midst.[viii] Years ago, the Spirit of God used this passage to teach me how to unlock the power of his kingdom. The key is submission (obedience). When we submit to the leadership of his spirit, it causes the Kingdom of God to take authority over every natural and physical law in the universe.

Obedience causes the miraculous power of God to flow upon any situation. Jesus fully understood the power of submitting to God. He submitted to God so perfectly that when the disciples asked Jesus to show them the father, Jesus said, if you have seen me, you have seen the father. He declared that he and the father were one. This does not mean that they are the same person. It means that they are one in mind and spirit; they are in agreement. They were in perfect alliance with one another. Because of Jesus' obedience, God made him the head of the church.

The church is called the Body of Christ; the hands and feet of Christ (the anointing) in the earth while Jesus reigns from heaven. When we are in agreement with God, we are in perfect union with his spirit. We are one with him; but when we as a body do our own thing we are as a house divided that is destined to fail. If the church fails, then the nations under its spiritual authority will also fail. The United States is faltering because the American church has squandered its spiritual authority in its rebellion against God.

Submission to the Spirit of God makes us perfect agents of God in the earth; who are capable of laying hold of all the power of heaven and manifesting that power for the benefit of men on this earth. Jesus was led in obedience by the Holy Spirit, and he told his followers to do the same. He told them that if they wanted to be his disciple, they had to *deny* their own desires by taking up their cross and follow his example.

Submission is God's desire for the church; that is why he is raising up his church in our midst. We are about to see God birth his sons in the earth; men and women of God who will do the works of God in perfect submission to his spirit. Many will say, "They think they are God." No. These are the sons of God; agents of God who walk, talk and act like God in the earth. It will be a sign and a wonder to behold these sons as they wield the power of heaven in the favor of the suffering masses of the earth. All people will marvel and glorify their father which is in heaven.

The State Of The Union (According To Heaven)

The American Church has amassed great wealth and political influence in the nation and in the world at large, Church growth has increased phenomenally. The fastest growing group of Christians in the country are charismatic and Pentecostals. It would seem that such church growth and influence would advance the Kingdom of God in America, but unfortunately the opposite is true.

The Spirit of God says that the American Church's relationship with him is similar to that of the Children of Israel as described in the Book of Judges. After the death of Joshua, there was such peace and prosperity, that future generations forgot the laws of God and went astray. No one remembered the warning given to Moses[ix] in which God promised that if the people would forget Him and turn to worship idols; they would perish and be driven from the land that God gave to them. With this warning, God said that is the people would seek him with all their hearts and souls; he would hear their cry and return them from captivity. Although God is a jealous and a consuming fire in rebuking his people, he also expressed his love and commitment to his covenant with them. God promised to show mercy to those who would turn from their wicked ways.

The Bible records numerous times when God's people forgot him and as result they were taken captive by their enemies. After being sorely oppressed by their enemies, they would cry out to God. God would hear their cry and send a deliverer to rescue the people and restore them to peace. Unfortunately, this was never the end of the story. The Children of Israel would have peace for about fifty years and then they would forget God again. Yet, God always had mercy upon them and restored them. This type of back and forth relationship with God has also been recorded in American history.

Many settlers came to the New World for a variety of reasons, but it was the Pilgrims and the Mayflower that captured the heart of what would be the spirit of America: family, faith and country. The Puritans wanted to create a pure and morally responsible society based upon the Bible. Everything they established was for this end; including the laws that governed everyday life; and the manner in which they educated their children. In fact, two of America's most prestigious colleges, Yale and Harvard Universities, were created by the Puritans as institutions of religious education for ministers and leaders of the colonies.

The Puritan influence is still evident in our Blue Laws today. Did you ever wonder why some businesses are closed on Sunday? Or why you cannot purchase alcohol on Sunday in many states? These states instituted laws reflect the Sabbath Day rest as prescribed by the Bible. Did you know that there are laws on the books stating that a person could be arrested and/or fined for committing adultery or sodomy? Remember Nathaniel Hawthorne's book *The Scarlet Letter*? Most Blue Laws are not being enforced, and would more than likely result in a legal battle over constitutionality.

Jim Crow laws are another reflection of our past. They were instituted after the Civil War and later replaced in the 1960's; but the effects of these laws are still evident in America, even in the American Church. Several years ago, there was a newspaper article about a legal dispute in the state of Virginia, where a couple wanted a civil marriage ceremony but was denied because blacks and whites could not marry according to Virginia law. This was a law instituted during slavery days. Laws change, but attitudes and hearts of men are slow to change. Years ago, I moved into an exclusive suburb of Kansas City. I worked in Missouri, and lived in Kansas. An advertising client aware that I was new to the area asked where I lived. When I told him he boldly asked, 'How did they let that happen?' I was appalled at his obvious racial overtones and he apologized. This man explained that in Kansas, there were Blue Laws stating that neither Blacks nor Jews could live in the area where I was living.

42

Even though no one attempted to enforce legal action against me, I did receive an unhealthy dose of racial comments and sneers from older residents who let me know that I was not welcomed in that city. Blue Laws were instituted during the mid 1600 to early 1700's. I n 1985, almost three hundred years later, there are people in America who were surprised that these laws were not being enforced. The racial condition of America stems directly from the racial tensions that continue to exist in the American Church where many *black only* and *white only* churches refuse to integrate. It has been said that Sunday morning is the most segregated time period in our country. This is a practice that began during slavery and it became more flagrant after the Civil War, even more throughout the days of Civil Rights marches in the 60's. After the Civil Rights Acts of 1964, racism did not go away, it became subversive; only in the American Church has it remained deliberate.

The Bible clearly states that in Jesus Christ all men are considered one in the Body of Christ.[x] And yet, religious attitudes in the Christian church since its beginnings in America have espoused both slavery and the separation of the races. God's heavenly kingdom consists of people from every tribe, tongue and nation.[xi] Preachers in America have long taught that God wanted the races separated and things came to a head in 1997 when the Spirit of God had Dr. Fredrick KC Price take on the issue in the pulpit. After much prayer and research, Dr. Price began a new teaching series entitled "Race, Religion and Racism."[xii] It was a powerful expository teaching on God's divine plan for the races, in particular his plan for the African, and African-American races. It was a positively motivating and uplifting series for anyone of any race, but the Christian hate mongers were spewing evil threats against Dr. Price's life. The Lord assigned me to intercede for Dr. Price and the church while the arrows of persecution hurled ferociously at him. This was the first time that I had experienced the level of hatred that existed among church leaders. It amazed me how men of God could step into the pulpit speaking about the love of God and then step out of the pulpit speaking murderous plots without remorse.

43

In volume one of this book, I mentioned some of the scenarios of hatred and racism that came against me while writing this book series. Racial hatred runs deep in the American Church much like it did during the Civil War when slavery bitterly separated our nation. Both the North and South believed that they were doing the will of God. The North wanted to abolish slavery and the South wanted it to remain; and both sides justified their positions with Bible scripture. As a nation, we have abolished slavery and we have declared that all men are equal; yet the church holds on to its right to remain racists; and they justify it with scripture.

There was a recent Christian radio interview with a well known prophet who claimed to have received a prophetic word from God in 2005 concerning who would be the next president in the 2008 election.[xiii] He was at a church meeting in Alabama when God spoke through him saying that America's next president would be a Black man. This prophet said that he was told not to tell anyone about his prophecy. Instead, these leaders began prophesying that God wanted other people to be president. Even when Barack Obama appeared came on the scene as a presidential candidate; this prophet said that God confirmed that this was our next president. This prophet only mentioned what happened in Alabama; and yet I personally remember rumors throughout the church about racial hatred hurled at leaders who voted according to God's instruction. Some pastors lost their jobs; some churches split. Leaders were offended because men chose to obey God rather than caving in to the pressure of their evangelical peers.

The radio interview continued with the host asking the prophet if electing a Black president lifts the curse of slavery off our nation. The prophet had a muddled answer. He said that America still had a race issue stemming from slavery, but it could only be cured if we repented for how we have treated Israel. This appeared to be another attempt to deny the slavery of our past with a Christian Zionist solution. As long as church leaders are in denial about their race issues stemming from slavery, the church will never be whole.

God deals with sin <u>directly</u>. If you lynch a man, God would have you repent for that murder and the hatred and anything else you have done that led to murder. It was though this prophet was telling America, "Yes, we know that you lynched and killed and enslaved Africans, but you must repent for not supporting Israel if you want forgiveness for murder and slavery." If politically supporting Israel was all we needed in order to have our sins forgiven and curses lifted; why did God send Jesus to the cross? This is further proof that laws change but attitudes and practices linger; dividing neighbors and brothers in the faith and in the nation. The Bible says that if we hate our brethren in the faith we are murderers and we will have no place in God's Kingdom.

Here is what the Spirit of God had to say on the issue of race. *We (America) need to repent for how we and our forefathers have mistreated nations and people that America has deceived, enslaved, terrorized and plundered in our zeal to possess world-wide territories, and/or commodities and resources necessary to protect and sustain our nation.* How soon have we forgotten not only what we did to the African slaves, but how we took land from Native Americans, killed millions through genocide and disease and enslaved others on reservations; how we stole Hawaii by overthrowing their monarchy with trickery. Not to mention the numerous people groups we have detain, incarcerated or deported because we deemed them to be a threat to our nation; whether they were an actual threat or not. Many of these people were born in this country but in the time of national conflict they were treated like traitors and enemies of the state. If we do not repent for what we have done to the nations of this world, the remnant of these nations will plunder us for the murder and violence we have caused in their cities and to those who dwell in them.[xiv] And this is just the beginning.

The Spirit of God also showed human blood flowing from the legislative to the judicial branches of the government throughout the country; indicating a deadly conspiracy or collusion against the people of our nation, and most cases directed a specific people groups. In the eyes of God, murder begins in the heart with a plot, or conversation with intent to malign or harm another without cause. This is called shedding innocent blood. Once the sin of murder is committed, God requires that one's own blood be shed as payment for shedding innocent blood.

There is another area of conflict among God's people which arises from the perceived differences between how America's government operates as opposed to that of God's government. America is a republic but most people see it as a democracy in which the majority rules. God's Kingdom is a monarchy and King Jesus is the only voice that rules over the government. The Spirit of God says there is rebellion in the church because people believe that the Kingdom of God should operate as a democracy like America. Therefore many churches are run as a democracy and ignore the governance and instruction of God.

This same misperception has led to misguided allegiances in the church. Many Christians esteem American values more sacred those prescribed by God for his Kingdom. These Christians would rather look to the federal government and its tax credits and free programs rather than seeking God for their true purpose in his Kingdom and operating by faith. Although the American dollar bears the words saying *In God We Trust*, American Christians are saying *In America We Trust*. Again, this is a conflict, but one that God blames on the American Church and its desire to rebel against him.

In the Kingdom of God, the church has been given all spiritual authority over the heavens and the earth. A rebellious church is one that is out of God's order; which means that everything under the church's authority is also out of God's order. It is no surprise that the government and many American businesses are faltering. What appears in the physical realm of the earth always begin with a spiritual seed that was sown. God has placed his people in every industry and branch of government in this country; not to earn a paycheck, but to hold down a kingdom military post as an intercessor. Where ever God places his people, there is a plan to prosper that organization. Christians by design are called to be innovators and people of excellence; but if we are rebelling against God, what was meant to be a blessing flowing out of our spirits, will instead become a curse upon everything we do. This is what happened to Adam in the Garden. He was created to bless and multiply creation causing it to prosper with God's abundance; but when he turn and did his own thing, he could only multiply the curse in the earth. The same thing is happening in America because the church has turned away from God.

The church will be held accountable for its stewardship over what God has given us. As a body, the church has done an admirable job in the area of rapidly responding to the aid of those suffering in national and world-wide catastrophes. Our emergency response is excellent, but our ability to provide preventative and/or corrective measures before a disaster is sorely lacking. Such actions require that the church spends time with God in prayer; waiting on the Holy Spirit to deliver instructions concerning coming events.

When Jesus left the earth, he said that he would leave the Holy Spirit to guide us and show us things that are to come. It is the Holy Spirit's job to show us dangers and opportunities that are approaching us. Unfortunately, many in the church, and especially evangelical churches, don't believe in the Holy Spirit. The Bible clearly demonstrates that Jesus was unable to perform a miracle, or endure severe persecution or the temptations of the devil without being led by the Holy Spirit.

As long as the church believes that the Holy Spirit is not necessary in our day, it will never be able to fulfill its purpose on earth; nor will it be able to clearly communicate the Gospel to the world. Because they do not believe in the supernatural power of God, signs and wonders will not follow the church. Signs and wonders were used by Jesus and his disciples to demonstrate the Gospel message. The supernatural signs included healing the sick, casting out demons, and causing the lame to walk and the blind to see. None of these signs can occur without the operation of the Holy Spirit. In our day of uncertainty, the world desperately needs someone who can hear from God and help the people prepare for coming events. God has always shown people major events before they happened. Before destroying the world with a flood, God told Noah to build an ark and to warn the people that disaster was coming. In the days of Sodom and Gomorrah, God told Abraham that he was going to destroy these cities, and he gave warning to Lot and his family, so they could escape disaster. When Joseph was a slave in Egypt, God gave him revelation knowledge about seven years of prosperity and seven years of famine coming to the land. God also gave him a plan of action to prepare enough food for the world during famine. Even before the events of 911, the Spirit of God alerted many people to start nation-wide prayer groups. The Holy Spirit will also give similar warnings about enemy plots against our families, business and churches as well. This type of sign would be a major demonstration of God's power and ability to transform an intended disaster into an instantaneous victory for his Kingdom. God has a solution for every event that will happen upon the earth. He is just waiting for his church to become obedient enough to His Spirit in order to show the power of the Kingdom. Instead, the church has rebelled. People argue that we are a Christian nation but that is not true. A Christian nation is one that espouses the teachings of Jesus Christ. We are a nation made up of many people professing to be Christian; but very few are actually following Jesus. In fact, few Christian churches still teach about Jesus or the Bible. If the church is confused about its identity in Christ, why should we be surprised that the nation is confused about Christianity and the Bible?

48

Many in the American church operate with an *us* versus *them* attitude when dealing with people outside of the church. This attitude has caused many churches to create communities in which there is virtually no contact with the non-Christian world. Some argue that *separation of church and state* requires that the church be isolated from the rest of the world. This is far from the truth. It was of utmost importance to our forefathers that the new government should stay out of their religious affairs. They did not want to be told by the government how they should practice their faith, and yet in America, those in the Christian faith do not have the freedom to fully practice their religion because of an erroneous interpretation of *the separation between church and state.* This is issue has not been adequately challenged because Christians have cowered in an attempt to be politically correct rather than standing up for what they know to be right. It is this same weak and wimpy church that Almighty God says is responsible for our faltering nation.

God placed the stewardship; the welfare and protection of this nation, in the hands of the church. We have failed miserably at being the salt and light in America. God has gifted us with his Spirit and wisdom enough to overturn every injustice in this nation and in the world. Jesus gave all power in heaven and earth to the church, and yet we sit back and watch as America has ignorantly uproots her own foundation in an attempt to separate from the God that gave her wealth, prosperity and power above all other nations of the world. If the foundation is destroyed, the nation falls; and the only hope for our nation is the church and God's Kingdom plan of action.

America has attacked God and Christianity as if she has found an unnecessary or loose thread that should be discarded. Her foolish actions have caused a chain reaction that will eventually unravel the very fabric of our nation; and yet God faults the church for not taking proper action to protect this nation from itself.

There will never be a complete separation between God and America. We are the only nation that was established by men and women who wanted a government that honored God. This has been clearly recorded in our country's history beginning with the Mayflower Compact.[xv]

Having undertaken, for the Glory of God and advancement of the Christian faith . . . a voyage to plant the first colony in the northern parts of Virginia, do by these presents solemnly and mutually in the presence of God and one of another, covenant and combine ourselves together into a civil body politic . . . '

When the Puritans came to establish the first colonies in America, they covenanted with one another and with God to dedicate this nation for glory of God and the advancement of the Christian faith. These settlers to the New World used the word *covenant*. They covenanted with God and with each other. Under Biblical Law, a covenant can never be broken; God honors covenants for a thousand generations.[xvi] God's promise of honoring the covenant will be good until Jesus returns and reclaims the earth for God's Kingdom.

Many Americans both native and naturalized still view America as a special blessing of God to the world. Early in our history people believed in *Providence*; that God was leading and guiding us through the formation and actualization of America. Today some call it *American Exceptionalism*; a special nation with a special destiny to lead the world. This exceptional distinction was divinely ordered by God. According to the Spirit of God, no other nation other than Israel has been so divinely created and anointed for his glory. So, whether we obey God or rebel against him, God will not utter destroy us. He will allow us to be prodded by enemy attacks until we fall back in line; just like he did with the Children of Israel. And so doing, America's example will lead the world back to righteousness.

The Case For War

"We wrestle not against flesh and blood, but against principalities, against powers, against the rulers of the darkness of this world, against spiritual wickedness in high places." Ephesians 6:12

The seat of war in America is the Christian Church; but all conflicts on earth have their root in one main spiritual cause: man's rebellion against God and his suffering the consequences of that rebellion. After Noah and the flood, God established the law of seed-time and harvest so that whatever a man sows that shall he also reap. If he sows to his flesh (things that look or feel good, or give one a sense of pride) then he will reap destruction. But if one sows to the spirit (according to the word and will of God), he will reap eternal life. [xvii]

In this chapter we will attempt to explain in brief the spiritual meaning behind the wars and conflicts on the earth. We will see their causes and the historical events that have led to war. The basic conflict is a battle between good and evil. God reaches out his loving hand with an inheritance for men on earth; while the unseen supernatural forces of evil wage a campaign of deception that penetrates the hearts and minds of human beings, causing them to rebel against God and short circuit their posterity. The tactic is a proven success for Satan and his demons. Most humans have no idea that they are pawns in a high stakes spiritual interaction. Many Americans both religious and secular are ignorant of activity in the spirit realm; choosing to only believe what they can see with their eyes, which is why they are reacting to issues rather living than proactively. In this chapter we will give Biblical reasoning for spiritual warfare and God's prophecy of how the troubles of the earth will end.

Military Mission Summary

Seat Of War: The Church (Individuals who keep the commands of God, and have the testimony of Jesus Christ)
Combat Zone: The United States of America

Reason For Conflict: Satan, being exiled to earth, declared war on the Church after learning that the inheritance Adam lost was returned to men on earth. This inheritance would allow anyone who believes in Jesus Christ to have dominion to subdue the earth, to replenish and multiply every resource necessary to sustain life on earth with heaven's infinite abundance. Satan has planted insurgents throughout the church and has launched extensive warfare against the entire human population of planet earth. Enemy deception and terror has stirred up strife, lawlessness, and wars, causing famine, sickness and death to run rampant across the earth. Satan's most successful tactic is posing as an Angel of Light; a religious or benevolent leader who gains the trust of unsuspecting masses, and then he steals, kills and destroys them all.[xviii] This deceiver is known as the Father of Lies.[xix] He has the uncanny ability to infiltrate the minds and hearts of the rebellious and emotionally wounded, with his army of powerful demons. The demonic intrusions target entire families and people groups in order to supplant God's purpose in the earth. These intrusions also utilized to create enemy strongholds that result in multiplied millions of human deaths. The ultimate goal of the enemy is to eliminate human beings before they have a chance to hear about God's inheritance. Satan know that any earthy human who would exercise his right to this inheritance could potentially cause multitudes of other humans to realize that God is love; that God is compassionate and gracious to his people; that God is good and God has plans for good and not evil, a plan for a future and a hope for every human on earth.

Military Strategy: The United States from its inception has been blessed by *Providence.* Because of America's faithfulness in honoring God, she has been exalted as a prominent world leader. America's wealth and superior strength has been long recognized by the nations of the world as evidence that God has blessed and favored her. Like the Biblical pattern of Israel, America has forgotten God and the enemy has been allowed to penetrate her borders. During the past fifty years, the country has legislated laws that are against the laws of God; and against the very values held by its people. This has resulted in an uprising of political and religious insurgents who have turned against God and the American government. These insurgents are disillusioned with the American dream that has been riddled with greed and corruption; and they are distrustful of the American church and its hypocrisy. The hope for America rests in the faith of a remnant of believers who know how much God loves this country. They know the grandiose plan of God for America; and they are willing to do what it takes to restore hearts back to God.

Strategic Goals: To launch all-out Kingdom assaults on enemy held-territories, in America and world-wide, with specific campaigns designed to release and empower those held captive by enemy regimes, and to occupy such territories till Jesus returns for his church. Campaigns would include:

1) Kingdom education, information and training (includes retraining for congregations who have been misled by false or incompetent teachers),

2) Kingdom power demonstrations by healing the sick, casting out demons, opening blind eyes, causing the lame to walk and raising the dead,

3) Kingdom resource distribution by multiplying scarce resources and discovering much needed new resources for human consumption,

Strategic Goals: (Continued)
   4) Kingdom cities powered by supernatural resources from heaven's operations,
   5) Kingdom discipleship training to train leaders who can duplicate this military strategy throughout the entire earth.

World-wide the Kingdom of God is suffering violence, but the violent are taking enemy territories by force.[xx] No longer will the nations be able to operate in their own power. God will establish his kingdom standard in America. Not only will it return her to a position of wealth, power and greatness; but it will transform the wealth and power of the nations. For God's Kingdom is supreme in wealth and power. God's Kingdom standard is impervious to enemy attacks of terror, poverty and devastation. While the kingdoms of this world will fail, the nations fortified by God's Kingdom will remain forever.

THE WAR STORIES AND THEIR MEANINGS

"O Beautiful For Heros Prov'd

In Liberating Strife.

Who More Than Self

Their Country Loved,

And Mercy More Than Life.

America! America!

May God Thy Gold Refine

Till All Success Be Nobleness

And Ev'ry Gain Divine."

3rd Stanza of *America The Beautiful* By Katharine Lee Bates
Public Domain: retrieved from
"http://en.wikisource.org//wiki//America_the_Beautiful"
Categories: PD-old-80-1923|Sheet music|1895 works

Issues Of Conflict: Our Social Disgrace

The truth of God is not tolerated within many American churches; therefore, some preachers have chosen a different audience. They have begun trying to enforce God's Word on the world at large by lobbying the legislature on social and moral issues they cannot even enforce within their own congregations. These are weak ineffective religious leaders have no respect in their own house; but they want tyrannical rule when dealing with people outside of their house. This external show of strength is an attempt to camouflage their leadership failures in the church. The biggest public deception in the *church* is its hypocrisy on social issues. Church leaders are notorious for trying to enforce God's law; knowing full well that neither they nor their congregations are walking in obedience to those same laws. What they say may be true according to the Bible, but it's like Jesus said about the Pharisees of his day, '*Do as they say but not as they do.* '[lxxi] These people will impose upon others strict rules that they themselves would never follow. The Spirit of God brought to my attention several areas of hypocrisy for this discussion: 1) homosexuality 2) abortion 3) bigotry 4) helping the poor and 5) support for Israel.

In *The War Journal (1999-2010) Volume I*, we mentioned issues of homosexuality, and abortion. Homosexuality is a political hot topic for Christian leaders, but you won't hear much rhetoric over the pulpit. What leaders are not talking about are the large numbers of homosexuals in the church. Most congregations pretend that they don't exist, while the house is buzzing with whispers, disapproving looks and innuendoes. This type of treatment causes homophobic dysfunction to flourish in the church. Another thing leaders are not talking about is the fact that many homosexuals are not the spiritual heathens the church depicts. They are people who desire to be part of the flock, if only the church would open up to them.

As an avid student of the Bible and a follower of Jesus Christ, I am convinced that if our Lord were on earth today, he would be spending his time with those whom the church rejects, and homosexuals would be a major part of his entourage of faithful followers. The conflict between the church and gays has escalated to heated political debate over Gay Marriage. In volume one of this book we covered God's view of gay marriage. God placed the desire for marriage inside of human beings. His idea of marriage is bigger than whether marriage should only be between one man and one woman. The Spirit of God said that the bigger issue is whether the marriage is in covenant with his will for the individuals involved. If God and his purpose are not at the center of the relationship, no marriage will last. It does not matter whether it is a heterosexual or a homosexual marriage, without God it will not last.

The Spirit of God is very grieved about this issue of gay marriage. He says that gays are desperately looking for love, and they have no idea that God is love. Rather than having compassion and showing gays the truth about God's love, the church has treated them with hatred. The Bible is clear that when anyone in the church speaks ill of another, God considers is as murder. The only weapon we need in order to commit murder is a tongue speaking words of hatred toward another person, especially if that person is a professed member of God's family. If we don't repent for this kind of hatred, you are considered a murderer; and there are no murderers in heaven.

The Spirit of God says that Christian leaders are trying to stone the gays just like they tried to stone the woman caught in the act of adultery. So why are they so anxious to stone the gays? These leaders attack gays to deflect attention away from their own sexual sins. Many pastors and leaders of the church have serious issues with pornography and sexual addictions.

God made it clear that the pornography and sex addiction flourishes in America because it is prominent in the church. Even the issues with homosexuality are on the rise because of their prevalence in the church. The Spirit of God simply says to the church; "Let him who has no sin cast the first stone at the gays." This is what Jesus told the religious leaders of his day who brought to him a woman that was *caught in the act* of adultery.[xxii] Jesus died so that we can be exonerated of our sins. So, if you have committed sexual sin or any other kind of sin against God, just ask him to forgive you. Then do as Jesus said to that woman accused of adultery; "Go and sin no more."

Sexual issues are not political; they are spiritual in nature. By making political propaganda out of these issues the church is shirking its responsibility. At a time when so many church leaders are complaining about "BIG GOVERNMENT" interfering in the lives of its citizens, why add to the government's responsibility *that* which God gave to the church? Morality should be taught in the church and reinforced in the home. Forcing the government to legislate moral issues is ludicrous. If the Laws of Moses could not keep people from sinning against God; what makes Christians think that the laws of the United States would do any better? Church leaders have also been very outspoken against abortion; but there would not be an abortion problem in America if Christian women would stop having abortions. It is preferable among Christian women to have an abortion than to suffer the public shame of an unwanted pregnancy. It is disturbing to hear that so many of these women refuse to follow God's position against abortion. Women who have had abortions suffer remorse and deep depression, even to the point of attempting suicide, but for the Christian who also knows that they have sinned against God, it can be quite severe. Far too many people in the church are suffering in the aftermath of abortion and no one is dealing with this issue.

Now, if you are a Christian who has had an abortion, God does not condemn you. Repent and let it go. Then forgive yourself and forgive those who were party to your decision to have the abortion(s). The beauty of God's grace is that our loving father is always waiting to pick us up when we fall. So it doesn't matter how many times we fall, God wants us to get up, get right and enjoy the joy of our salvation.

If you are having lingering difficulty with guilt and depression after an abortion, seek professional counseling. It is important to find one with a heart of compassion and an understanding of Biblical principles of life and healing: someone who would also be willing to pray for you. In volume one of this book, we recorded how the Spirit of God viewed abortion. He said that sinners kill babies because they don't know God, but his greatest concern is for believers who abort the seed of his word. Please understand God does not approve of murdering babies; but it hurts him even more when we take his seed of salvation, and then turn back to do our own thing. Innocent lives are taken daily, but Jesus *gave his life* so that we could have a chance of living a life and purpose that glorifies God.

In the eyes of God, conception does not begin in the womb of the mother; life begins in the spiritual womb of God. The Lord told the prophet Jeremiah that *before* he was in his mother's womb. God had a plan and purpose for his life.[xxiii] The Apostle Paul revealed to believers that God chose us to be In Him (God's family through Jesus Christ) *before* the foundation of the world. God predestined us to be his adopted children.[xxiv] God is a good father who has only thoughts of peace toward us, not evil. God wants to give us wonderful future and hope.[xxv] When we turn from God after accepting Jesus and the seed of salvation, it is willful rejection of the cross and the redemption it offers. For the Christian, abortion is not a social or political issue; it's a spiritual one in which God will hold us accountable, if we do not repent.

The next issue of concern: is how the church treats the poor and people of color in America. The evangelical movement has a history steeped in bigotry against poor, uneducated, people of color including Black, Africans, and Jews. Evangelicals pride themselves for having advanced theological degrees and honors. These seminary trained theologians thoroughly research the Bible, but have limited or no experiential knowledge in the things of God. So feeding the hungry or taking care of the poor is beneath what they believe God is calling them to do. The wealthier the congregations, the more out of touch these leaders are with the real world around them. These congregations arrogantly dismiss the poor, or hurting or even the sick or uneducated as those who are lazy. Rather than giving a helping hand to those in need, they are more likely to send them to a social service agency or to the county government for assistance. This is totally against what God desires for his people.

Evangelical leaders complain that the government is spending too much money on poor and unemployed people. Not many of these leaders are offering programs to relieve this area of government spending. In fact, they are not offering any solutions at all, only political rhetoric. Often these leaders will claim that poor people don't have the Christian work ethic, and if they don't work, they don't eat. So, Christian leaders will not help them, nor will they feed them. This is completely opposite of what the Bible teaches and what Jesus demonstrated. Therefore God will make the church pay for this disobedience.

Another abuse of the church is their bigotry toward those who are different. There is a clear attempt by evangelical leaders to poison the minds and hearts of people by using toxic labels that mask their hatred of certain people groups such as *Islamic Terrorist, Communists and Communism, Socialist and Socialism.* These are terror tactics used to invoke fear among people; and yet the Bible tells us not to fear men.

Historically, similar tactics have been used by the church to promoted racists and sexist ideology. Fortunately the American public is smart enough to see through such manipulative maneuvers. Church folk, on the other hand, can be easily swayed. Be reassured of one thing. Jesus died for all men; that includes the Islamic terrorist, the communists and the socialists. We are commanded to pray God's will that all men are saved and come into the knowledge of truth.

We end this chapter with a brief discussion of the church's view of Israel. There are some American churches that are anti-Semitic. They believe that when the Jews rejected Jesus as Messiah, God somehow cut them off forever. This is not true. The Bible clearly states that God has allowed the gentiles to be grafted into the family of God , but the Jews will finally recognized Jesus and acknowledge him as their Messiah.[xxvi]

Another group of Christian leaders has become a Pro Israel lobbying group in Washington D.C. While in prayer about this chapter, the Spirit of God had some very strong comments about what the American Church should be doing to support Israel. The Spirit of God said, *"Leave Israel Alone."* He also reminded me that Christians are commanded to pray for the peace of Jerusalem,[xxvii] but we are to stay out of the political issues over land rights. There are two specific reasons God says to leave Israel alone. First of all, he said that Christians are trying to make the Biblical prophecies concerning Israel come to pass. He said that Christians are doing what Sarah did in trying to bring God's word to past in her life. God promised Sarah and Abraham that they would have a child. In Sarah's mind, she was past the child bearing age and could not have a child. So, she offered her servant Hagar to Abraham to produce a child to fulfill this prophecy.[xxviii]

God knew how old Sarah and Abraham were when he made the promise. Why didn't Sarah wait for God's plan to bring the promise to past? She interpreted the prophecy with her human understanding. This is exactly what Christians are doing in lobbying for Israel. They have the Bible and are trying to make the United States go along with what the prophecy says. This is not how God works. He doesn't need our help anymore than he needed Sarah's help. Sarah interfered with God's plan and created Ishmael who has been a thorn in the side of Israel even to this day. *"Leave Israel Alone,"* and if God said it, he will surely bring this and all prophecies concerning Israel to past.

The second reason God said to leave Israel alone has to do with the motive behind some of the lobbyists. Some American leaders have not followed the instruction of God concerning their own ministries, yet they will support Israel in hopes that God will give them a special blessing. In doing so, these leaders are honoring men before honoring God. Others will sacrifice money to legally and politically support Israel, while neglecting the poor and suffering in America. They have become Pro Israel in their acts of service, and Anti American in their neglect of the poor. These people hate the so called "American welfare state" and they think God will give them a special blessing just because they support Israel. God calls these actions *"Anti-American"* in thought and deed. The Bible says that obedience is better than sacrifice. Rebellion is like the sin of witchcraft and stubbornness is like iniquity and idolatry. Because they rejected the word of God, God will also reject them, if they do not repent.[xxix]

God planted churches and ministries in America for one purpose: TO OCCUPY TILL JESUS COMES! Men and women of God are called to do kingdom business where God has planted them, yet many refuse to obey because they think they have better ideas for *their* ministries. They fail to understand that the basic service in American Christianity is supposed to be caring for the poor, the widow, the father less and the stranger *within* our borders.

65

There is a special blessing attached to the caring of those in need. It is a subject very dear to the heart of God and it is a constant theme throughout the Bible. God loves people and the church is the only organism ordained to demonstrate that love through our obedience to his word. It is our duty as Christians to fear God and to keep his commandments, because God will bring every works into judgment. We will be judged for everything; whether it's good or bad, seen or unseen. God knows all and will judge us all.[xxx]

Unlawful Enemy Combatants

Throughout this book we encounter issues involving conflicts between God and man. Most humans would say that God does not understand how modern man thinks and operates in this world. God would say that man does not understand how <u>He</u> thinks and operates in the world that <u>He</u> created. Oh, the arrogance of intelligent men who would dare instruct Almighty God! Where were they when God created the foundations of the Earth? Did they instruct him then? When God fashioned human beings after his image and likeness, did men have any input? Are men like the immortal God who has observed the seasons and behavior of men since the beginning of time? NO! So, what gives men the authority to tell God how things should work in the earth?

Pride and arrogance in the hearts of men gives them the self-appointed authority to become their own gods. Yet, God told the prophet Jeremiah that the human heart is deceitful above all things, and it is desperately wicked. But who can know what's in the heart of man? Only God knows. He continued by telling Jeremiah that he (God) searches the hearts of men and will reward every man according to what He does.[xxxi] This is perhaps the most detrimental issue that faces the American church. It is unaware of just how evil the human heart is towards God. Jesus Christ offers men an opportunity for a heart transformation. He then commands us to love the Lord our God will all our heart in order to be pleasing to God. We are also told to put God first and he will place his desires in our hearts. Unfortunately, the American church has the mistaken belief that God wants to make us happy and will give us the desires of our evil hearts. So Americans pray and receive nothing from God because they don't ask for the will of God for their lives. Instead, they pray for things that fulfill the lust of their hearts. God will not answer these prayers.

The American church is warring against its members in order to satisfy the lust of its heart. This is a major corruption in the church. Instead of adopting and developing the heart of God as demonstrated by Jesus Christ, the church has promoted a self-motivated and personal benefit gospel that strives for the American dream of wealth, self-sufficiency and prestige. This false gospel is self-promoting and does not include the key aspects of Jesus' ministry such as healing the sick, and feeding the poor. According to God, a wicked heart is an incurable sick heart; a malignancy leading to death. The condition of one's heart is of upmost importance to God. The heart is the calibration device that determines how much of God's supernatural power will work through an individual. Ephesians 3:20 identifies the ideal heart conditions under which the Lord will perform exceedingly, abundantly above all one can ask or think. This work can only be done according to the power of God that is allowed to work through the individual's heart.

The light of the body is the eye (heart), if your heart is single-minded in God; the body will be full of light. If the eye (heart) is evil against God, the body will be full of darkness. In volume one of this book, we had numerous journal entries that described how church leaders had an evil eye against God. Some of these leader's hearts were completely black and full of hate. The leaders were hateful and jealous because God was answering the prayers of the congregations, but the preachers couldn't get a prayer through for themselves. In retaliation for not getting what they wanted from God, many leaders decided to take matters into their own hands. No longer did they trust God to get what they wanted, they took it upon themselves to kill, steal and destroy God's people. As James 1:27 says, they asked and did not receive because they'd rather get it themselves than to ask God properly. And those who asked did not receive from God because they asked to satisfy their lust.

Why would a man or woman of God continue operating in the church when they have become jealous of God's people and no longer desire to submit to the word of God? Bible promises are contingent upon our obedience. Why won't these leaders just repent for their anger and begin obeying God? The answer to these questions is specific to the individual, however, in my experience, these types of leaders they tend to rationalize their sin. The attitude behind their thinking is very religious and judgmental in nature. They display arrogance even while operating in sin. They have no fear of God. They have no fear of man. They are blinded by their evil hearts and feel justified in remaining that way. These people may have joined a church and become a leader, but they never received the love of God, nor do they recognized the goodness of God in their lives. Their behavior is similar to an injured or wounded animal that will bite the hand of anyone wanting to help alleviate their pain

And, so the battle continues. God's leaders are warring against God and as if they are fighting against the devil. They call good evil and evil good and wonder why God won't answer their prayers. Self-deceived and Hell bound, these leaders are perpetrators of their own doom.

Jesus told his disciple that men would hate them and try to kill them. They do so because they don't know God or Jesus Christ whom he sent. They did the same to Jesus during his day. If we are to be like our master, then we must endure persecution like he did.

Until evil hearted people want to be healed, they will continue to create strife and destroy others. How often it has been said that hurting people will hurt other people. It's what they do. It's a choice that they've made even though they are fully aware that God offers betters options that result in blessings and not curses. The church is filled with hurting people who walk in the curse, yet they blame God and others for their sorrows. These self-deceived souls would rather go to Hell than give up their evil hearts. The Bible says that as a man thinks in his heart, so he will be in life. It should be no surprise that if out of the treasures of their evil hearts they begin to manifest evil in all they say and do. According to their faith, so it will be done until them.

God's System Of Justice

After the flood in Noah's day, God made a covenant with man and beast of the earth. God promised that he would never completely destroy both man and beast as he did when the waters flooded the earth. God also promised never to curse the ground as he did because of the evil hearts of men on earth. Beloved, God is no longer causing the destruction in the earth. It is the law of seed-time and harvest that is in operation.[xxxii] Like the law of gravity, seed-time and harvest has been incorporated in the earth. So, rather than God punishing man for his evil heart, man determines his own fate and suffers the consequences of his choices. Therefore, the destruction we see in the earth is because men have allowed it to exist. Our Lord is a God of Justice. He executes justice for the poor, the widow, the fatherless, the orphan and the stranger. He also executes justice for all who cry out to him. Those who trust him shall never be made ashamed of their hope in his justice. *"Vengeance is mine; I will repay saith the Lord."*[xxxiii]

So what does God's justice look like? The Psalmist David tells how God delivered him from death at the hands of King Saul: *"In my distress I called upon the Lord, and cried unto my God: he heard my voice out of his temple, and my cry came before him, even into his ears. Then the earth shook and trembled; the foundations also of the hills moved and were shaken, because he was wroth."*[xxxiv] This is how David described his deliverance from death. What we know about this Psalm is was during the time that King Saul pursued and encamped against David at Ziph (I Samuel 26). David had a chance to kill Saul, but he refused to touch God's anointed. Because David honored God and King Saul, the Lord delivered him from death.

In the Preface of this book we mentioned the prophecy from December 2010 in which the Spirit of God said that the shaking in the earth was due to the suffering of the obedient sons of God. As these sons prayed and obeyed God, it was causing the earth to shake all that was not in accord with God's plan and purpose.

This is essentially what we saw in the case of David. God declared him King of Israel and because of the opposition from the reigning King Saul, God had to shake both the heavens and the earth to bring his word and his Son David into his rightful place on earth.

For God's justice to occur in our lives, we must obey God and allow him to lead our lives, and leave vengeance to him. As we do, God will turn the world upside down just to accommodate his obedient sons. When we believe God and obey no matter what comes against us, God will manifest himself in our situation and turn things in our favor; in ways we could have never imagined.

We just discussed God's justice for his obedient sons, but what does it look like for everyone else? We mentioned that God will do justice for anyone who cries out to him like David did. But what happens if a person does not know to cry out? Can or will God do justice for them? The answer is yes. God's system of justice is much like ours in that someone must make a plea before a judge before injustice can be corrected. God is the judge. If a person cannot cry out for themselves, God will in his wisdom choose an intercessor to cry out on the behalf of the one in danger. The best example of this in the Bible was when God told Abraham that he was going to destroy the city of Sodom.[xxxv] The cries of injustice were very great against Sodom and Gomorrah and God was sending angels to investigate. Abraham's nephew Lot lived in Sodom with his family. Hearing God's plan to destroy the city prompted Abraham to bargain with God to save the righteous ones in the city. The angels went to Sodom and got Lot and his family out, and then the city was destroyed with fire and brimstone. Lot had no clue that the city was to be destroyed. God let Abraham know the judgment against Sodom and Gomorrah knowing that he would ask to spare the Lot's life. Therefore, Abraham became an intercessor prompted by God to spare another's life from danger.

Another example of intercession was when Job's friend's stir up the wrath of God against themselves. God commanded them to make a sacrifice and go to Job to pray for them.[xxxvi] Because Job was a righteous man and acceptable before God, the only way the wrath would be satisfied was through Job's prayers of intercession for his friends. In these two examples, it was God who prompted the prayers of intercession. A non-believer can go to a righteous person and ask for intercession in an issue. The Bible also encourages believers to pray for one another. James 5:16 says that *"the effectual fervent prayer of a righteous man availeth much."* I Peter 3:12 also says that ". . . the eyes of the Lord are over the righteous and his ears are open to his prayers.

We mentioned that judgments are built within our physical and spiritual realm for those who violate the laws of the earth. Anyone would agree that the law of gravity holds whether or not you agree to its existence. If you walk off a bridge, you will fall. Yet men and women walk off spiritual bridges all day long and they fall; and they think this is just the way life is supposed to be. If someone fell off a physical bridge you would think he is crazy or distraught over some situation. When people fall spiritually, people rarely notice and others don't care. Many people fall off bridges into divorce, drugs, poverty and sickness even after knowing that similar fates have taken their parents and others in their blood line. These judgments indicate a generational curse; caused by a sin or iniquity that has been perpetuated in a family bloodline.

Consider them cancer cells in the spiritual bloodline. If a person is diagnosed with a physical form of cancer, there would be efforts to find the cause and a cure. Treatment would most likely be prescribed before someone would naturally succumb to cancer. Yet, no one seems interested in diagnosing or treating signs of deadly spiritual cancers that affect our lives. Some are ignorant of what can be done. Others have resigned themselves to live and die of the very sickness and disease that they inherited from their parents. As a result, the judgment of God in the form of a curse is passed on to another generation.

In the Kingdom of God, believers have been given authority over all the power of the enemy. We are commanded to heal the sick and to cast out demons, to restore peace and health to our fellow man. If I know that you are suffering from cancer and I possess the cure but I don't share it with you; God would hold me responsible because He gave me that cure for you. God wants you free, but if you reject the cure God will not hold me responsible.

God is a God of justice; and he hates all oppression. Acts 10:38 says that God anointed Jesus with the Holy Ghost and power so that he could go about doing good and healing all who were oppressed by the devil. The Bible says repeatedly, that God is the defender of the poor, the fatherless, the widow, the stranger, those without families, children and all who are helpless to defend themselves. The Spirit of God has had me in prayer focusing on world-wide oppression; very serious oppression that has been suppressed and hidden underground in the world of pornography, sex slavery, and extortion. God is about to shut these operations down and take revenge on the behalf of all whom have suffered because of this evil. We are in the hour of God's vengeance and he will be setting the captives free. The Spirit of God has declared that it is time to comfort all who mourn.

Dividing The Spoils

"I will give thee the treasures of darkness and the hidden riches of secret places." Isaiah 45:3

When God takes revenge, he rescues those who suffer and punishes the evil parties. God also gives financial relief to the innocent. We saw this when the Children of Israel were enslaved in Egypt. God heard their cries and sent Moses to deliver them out of bondage. They were not only freed, but they plundered Egypt of all its wealth. What we are about to see in this hour will be similar to what happened in Egypt. God will bring such horror upon his enemies that they will pay the people of God to depart from them. When it ends, the people of God will be left standing, holding it all. God will see that his people plunder their enemies. The Spirit of God talked to me about making restitution for wrongdoing against his people. What he showed me was not only restitution, there were punitive damages awarded in many instances, just to make a public example out of God's enemies.

Many in the Body of Christ always believed that one day God would take wealth of the wicked and give it to the just; and that is also about to happen in our midst. You might ask why God would do such a thing. The answer is simple. The Kingdom of God is about to be established in the earth before Jesus returns. In this prophet's estimation, we may have another fifty years before Jesus breaks forth in the clouds with power and great glory. In the meantime, the sons of God have to prepare the way by rescuing the poor and suffering masses. These are the victims of government and institutional systems that now exist. In a prophecy I received in December 2010, the Spirit of God vowed that he was shaking every foundation in this earth in preparation for Jesus' return. For any systems to survive they will have to be converted to God's kingdom operations. God's Kingdom is the only refuge from the shaking and violence that will be ever increasing in frequency and intensity.

God is going to make sure that his people are equipped with every financial resource available to implement his plan for the earth. His plans are disaster proof and they are beneficial to all men. No longer will there be a disparity among the rich and the poor. God's people will see that all men have all they need to survive and thrive in this final hour of earth's existence. There will be world governments, education systems, industry and business alliances that will flourish under God's Kingdom plan. God's plan for man will be finally realized in the earth; a life of endless blessings and abundance.

In addition to seeing the wealth of the wicked transferred to the righteous, we are going to see God's people producing ideas and concepts, new inventions and innovative products that will cause the economies of the world to flow once again. Think it not strange that all the governments of the world are faltering financially. This is by design. The wisdom of men is limited; but the wisdom of God is eternal; his design for the earth is that of increase. God's Kingdom only advances in multiplicity; it never falters.

For those who refuse to convert to God's Kingdom plan, there will great pain and suffering; but for those who flow with God it will be an ever increasing supply of blessings and supernatural abundance. For the masses who have suffered, it will be a welcomed relief. We will see first-hand what it's like when the righteous are in authority and the people rejoice; and rejoice they will for the abundance of goodness and mercy that God has in store for those who have been faithful to him!

CONCLUSION

"The Lord Bringeth The Counsel Of The Heathen
To Nought: He Maketh The Devices Of People
Of None Effect.

The Counsel Of The Lord Standeth Forever,
The Thoughts Of His Heart to All Generations.

Blessed Is the Nation Whose God is The Lord;
And The People Whom He Hath Chosen
For His Own Inheritance.

There Is No King Saved By The Multitude Of An Host:
A Mighty Man Is Not Delivered By Much Strength.

An Horse Is A Vain Things For Safety:
Neither Shall He Deliver Any By His Great Strength.

Behold, The Eye Of The Lord Is Upon Them That Fear
Him, Upon Them That Hope In His Mercy;
To Deliver Their Soul From Death,
And To Keep Them Alive In Famine."

Psalm 33:10 12, 16-19 KJV

Enduring Hardship Like A Good Soldier

The message to God's people in this hour is to endure until the end. We can expect hardships to increase in the world, but those who endure to the end will be saved. In an earlier chapter we talked about suffering for righteousness sake. Just like God chose Jesus to suffer on the cross, Christians are also chosen to deny themselves, take up their crosses and follow him. As Christians, our cross is the individual believer's suffering that is a result of their obedience to God. It's the suffering of a martyr; one who has given all for the cause of the Kingdom. Some give of themselves, even to death. Others are called to stand in spite of persecution, death threats and enemy retaliation.

Suffering is not a popular subject of discussion in the American church. If Christians don't want to obey God in the simple things, how can they be convinced to suffer in the hard things? How often American Christians take for granted that we live in a country where it is not illegal gather in a church; or teach about Jesus; or even carry a Bible. Many of our brethren in other nations risk their lives while practicing their faith. Unfortunately Americans have viewed *martyrdom* as something that is done in other countries; but God expects us to live as martyrs for Jesus Christ. We are to give up everything for the sake of the kingdom.

After Jesus' resurrection, he appeared to his disciples and told them that when the Holy Ghost comes they receive power to be a witness for him.[xxxvii] This term witness is also used to describe martyrs who are witnesses of Jesus Christ who remain faithful until death. The Lord has also taught me much about the purpose in suffering. It's not a pleasant topic; but it is a topic that shrouds a mystery of God's blessings and his power. Jesus suffered on the cross for the joy of something that God revealed in his purpose. When God calls us to suffer, it's not about us; it's about God's purpose in the lives of men on earth. This type of suffering takes your faith to another level of maturity. It requires that you take your eyes off of your pain and look to Jesus who suffered so much more for our sakes. This is the ultimate call to lay down your life for a friend.

A good warrior learns how to suffer well. There were recent days in which I didn't know if I could finish my assignment because I grew tired of staring death in the face. The only relief I got from the Spirit of God was, *Be faithful till death*. Then I got a revelation that death had no power over me. Jesus arose from the grave and announced that he had all power in heaven and earth. He then gave that power to believers and told us to go into the world demonstrating that power and teaching nations about the kingdom.

When we are faithful to God, he will take revenge upon those who come against us. In the prophecy entitled, "The Foundations are Shaken," the Spirit of God admonished his martyrs to remain faithful because in this faithfulness, the entire earth was being shaken right side up. In our suffering the fullness of God's power is birthed in our spirit. It's as if we are becoming super human beings in the process of suffering. This is what happened to Jesus. He overcame the suffering of the cross and even death and hell; and he emerged with all power heaven, earth, death and hell. When we suffer through something for the sake of the kingdom, we are actually taking the power away from the one who tried to destroy us. Jesus said that he had given us authority over all the power of the enemy. In our suffering, we can lay hold of that power; and when we possess that power, we can then go into the world and free others.

Oh, believer in Jesus Christ, I exhort you to remain faithful to him until death. If we love Jesus, we will obey his commands. Love bears all things, believes all things; hopes in all things, endures all things.[xxxviii] I admonish you in the same manner that the Apostle Paul admonished Timothy: to endure hardship like a good soldier. He also told him to endure all things for the sake of the elect that they may also obtain salvation. He closes his admonition by comparing our suffering to that of Jesus Christ. *If we died with him, we will also live with him. If we endure, we will also reign with him. If we deny him, he will also deny us; if we are faithless, he will remain faithful, he cannot deny himself.*[xxxix]

82

Don't Be Entangled In Civilian Affairs

Believers in Jesus Christ are called to be soldiers for the Kingdom. A good soldier cannot get involved in the cares and distractions of this life and expect to be effective on the battle field; nor would you want to go to battle with someone whose mind was not on the enemy at hand.

These are the last days, and Jesus told us to watch and pray and not let the cares of the world be a snare for us. If there is something that we need, the Lord promises to supply our needs according to his riches in glory. Cast your cares on the Lord and make your request known to him and let it go. He promises that if we seek first the Kingdom of God and his righteousness all the things we need will be given to us.

Let go of every weight (people, things, emotions and thoughts) that are counterproductive to your assignment. Put away lasciviousness, drunkenness and all sin for good. Stay focused on the task at hand. You are in an intense battle of life and death. Remain faithful to your Commander and Chief, and your fellow comrades.

Jesus has commissioned us to go into all the world to teach nations the gospel. Take the word of faith and wage a good warfare until the mission is completed. Where ever you are stationed, occupy until Jesus returns, so that you may please him who has chosen you to be an honorable soldier in his military. He who began a good work in you is faithful to complete it. Obey your orders soldiers; and look forward to hearing *"Well done my good and faithful servant."*

Contend Lawfully For The Prize

The book of Revelation portrays the wrath of God, plagues and the final battle between Jesus and Satan on the earth in graphically frightening detail. There is constant debate as to whether the visions in Revelation are allegories or descriptions of real events that are to come. Preachers often avoid talking about this important book of the Bible either because they don't understand it or they fear that congregations will not understand. Even though it may be overwhelming to read, it is important for every believer to read and pray for God to give them understanding about events that are soon coming to this earth. When the Apostle John received these visions from God, he was commanded to speak the message of Revelation to the church as a warning of things to come. John also said that there is a blessing for all believers who read and obey the words of the book of Revelation. Conversely, the book ends by pronouncing a curse on anyone who alters the words of this book. This curse could be part of the reason preachers are fearful of teaching on this book. But it is probably the most useful book to the believer because Revelation not only tells what is to come, but it tells what God expects from us. It also tells us who will and will not qualify to be in heaven, thereby giving each of us the opportunity to repent and fall in line with God's word. Therefore the blessing is in the fact that even though wrath is coming, God is giving the church a way of escape from the wrath. This is a blessing from God indeed.

One of the most powerful blessings of Revelation is that it clarifies who will enter heaven. At first glance, the reader may overlook the fact that this book is written for believers. Most Christians automatically assume that they will automatically go to heaven. John 3:16 says that God gave his only begotten son so that whoever believes in him *should not perish*. God, through his son Jesus offers all men the opportunity to partake in everlasting life, but it is conditional. You must obey God by believing in Jesus. Believing is a heart issue. Romans 9:10 says that if we confess with our mouth the Lordship of Jesus and believe in our hearts that God raised him from the dead, we will be saved.

A person can only confess with their mouth, that which they believe in their heart. For out of the abundance of the heart, the mouth speaks. How do you know if a person truly believed in his or her heart, and didn't repeat empty words? Only God knows for sure who among us will be with him in heaven, and who will draw back. The Bible says that the enemy plants tare (false brethren) among the wheat (true believers). The tare is allowed to remain with the wheat until the final harvest at which time; the tare will be separated and burnt in the fire. Jesus also claimed that there will be many people calling him Lord, but he will only recognize those who did the will of the father. All others will be cast out of the kingdom and Jesus will say 'depart from me you workers of iniquity, I never knew you.'

Revelation 21:8 gives a list of people who will not be in heaven: the fearful and unbelieving, the abominable, murderers, whoremongers, sorcerers, idolaters, and all liars will have their place in the lake of fire. Now remember the book of Revelation was written for the churches, so this passage confirms that not all who are in the church are in the kingdom. The Lord said that he that overcomes shall inherit all things and the Lord will be his God and the overcomers will be his sons. Several years ago, the Lord demonstrated to me the seriousness of Revelation 21:8. I was out with a friend who is a powerful woman of God. I trusted her because of her love for God and love for God's people. It was a time of transition for me this friend promised to do something for me that was vital to my assignment. As she vowed to do this thing, my heart was grieved because I knew she was lying. I believe that she wanted to do the thing in her heart, but we both were aware that her husband would never let her do what she was offering to do. Her husband hated the church and was very abusive. While she was speaking to me face-to-face, I began speaking to God in my heart I asked the Lord why she lied and offered to do something that she knows her husband would never permit her to do.

In an instant, the Spirit of God put a word in my mouth shook us both. *"All liars will have their part in the Lake of Fire."* We both trembled as these words came out of my mouth. My friend repented on the spot. I remember getting a Bible and pulling out this passage and the Lord confirmed that this message was for those in the church. Even for the tongue-talking, miracle working saints. None of us are exempt from these words. She and I asked God to search our hearts for anything that would disqualify us from spending an eternity with him. How horrifying it was to us to know that after all we have done for God and his kingdom, that we could ourselves be disqualified if our hearts held onto sin. The Lord showed us that having head knowledge of the word will not save us. The word must be in our hearts, only then can we walk worthy of the calling he has set before us.

In Matthew 10:22, when Jesus described destruction coming to the earth at the end of this age, he said that he that endured to the end would be saved. If we receive Jesus and turn back, there is no more payment for sins. That means we will have to pay with our lives and suffer the fiery consequences of judgment. Once we come into the kingdom of God we must live by our faith. Without faith, it is impossible to please God. He finds no pleasure in those who turn back. It is to our benefit that we seriously count the cost of following Jesus. He is expecting each of us to take up our cross to follow him. The cross is the battle required for you to successfully endure your walk of faith. Everyone is assigned a cross to bear, but not everyone takes up their cross because they don't like to suffer. And, many were told that when they came to faith in Jesus, their lives would be easy. So, now they are unwilling to go into battle for their salvation. They question if Jesus defeated the devil then why do I have to fight. We are to occupy till he returns. Jesus defeated the enemy; we are placed on earth as part of a peace keeping mission. We are occupying the territory and ensuring that Satan's power remains crippled.

We are expected to reign on this earth by our faith, but if we put our hand to the plow to do a job for the kingdom and turn back, we are not fit for the kingdom. For believers in Jesus Christ, we want to stir up your minds to remember all that has been spoken and written about the things to come. The Lord does not want any of us to perish, but he wants us to repent. We are in the last days of this world and Jesus will return for his church and then the wrath of God will finally destroy all the enemies of God. Given this, we admonish you to be diligent in the things God has committed to your care, so that you may be found in peace without spot and blameless before Him. If you have never given your heart to Jesus and would like to be among those who avoid the wrath of God, you can do so right now. Just pray the following and let God through his Holy Spirit have full control of all you say and do from this day forth.

Dear God in Heaven,

I repent for trying to live my life without you. I repent of all sin. I renounce Satan and all the works of darkness that I have committed against you to this day. From now on I want your son Jesus to be Lord; master and ruler of my life. I believe that Jesus arose from the dead and that same resurrection power can transform every area of my life. I want that power now. Please fill me with your Holy Spirit. I want him to lead and guide me to your perfect will for my life. Holy Spirit, please teach me how to abide in God's word so that all the goodness of God's kingdom will manifest in my life, so that I can walk worthy of being called a son (or daughter) of God. Thank you Father for this free gift of salvation and I received it In Jesus' Name. Amen.

If you just read this prayer; we welcome you into the family of God. Read your Bible and spend time in prayer daily. Find a Bible teaching church family and enjoy your new life in Jesus Christ (See Appendix for helpful references). Let the Holy Spirit lead you into the greatest adventure of your life.

APPENDIX

OTHER RESOURCES

Websites For Free Online Bibles:
Ethnic Harvest   www.ethnicharvest.org/bibles/
(Parallel language bibles in over 250 languages)

The Blue Letter Bible   www.blueletterbible.org
(Reading, study tools and commentaries)

The Bible Gateway   www.biblegateway.com
(International versions w/commentaries)

Audio Version of Bible   www.audio-bible.com
(Read and listen to King James Version with special tools for the
visually impaired)

To Order A Personal Copy Of The Bible:
Faith Comes By Hearing   www.faithcomesbyhearing.com
(Free mp3 downloads in over 400 languages, or Purchase digital
audio players loaded with the Bible)

Free Bible Ministry   www.getyourfreebible.com
(For Residents of Africa and Philippines only)

Free Bible   www.freebibles.net
(For sick, poor or imprisoned individuals in the US—allow 4-6
weeks)

To Order Large Quantities Of Bibles For Personal Or Ministry:
The American Bible Society   www.americanbible.org

Biblica Direct   www.ibsdirect.com

i

HOW TO FIND A BIBLE TEACHING CHURCH

The best source of information about churches in your area is the people you know. If you don't know anyone that goes to church, then feel free to use the following resources.

The Believer's Voice Of Victory Network (BVOVN)
Kenneth Copeland Ministries
Fort Worth, Texas 76192
Prayer Line (877) 281-6297
http://www.kcm.org/church-listing

Trinity Broadcasting (TBN)
PO Box A, Santa Ana, CA   92711
24hr Prayer and Request Line (714)731-1000, (888)731-1000
www.tbn.org/contact/

Christian Broadcasting Network (CBN)
977 Centerville Road, Virginia Beach, VA 23463
24hr Prayer Line (800)759-0700
www.cbn.com   (Search Church Finder)

Or better yet, pray about it and let the Spirit of God lead you to a church. It may indeed be a denominational church and the only church in your area.

Just remember, no matter where you choose to go, it's not about the church or the people, it's about your relationship with God, the Father. So, go to church to fellowship with like minded believers, but spend the rest of the week communing with God and reading His word.

MORE FROM THE AUTHOR

Paula Matthews is an author and speaker whose prophetic writings have captured the attention of many enthusiastic followers after the initial release of *The War Journal (1999-2010) Volume* I in 2010. The book spawned dozens of online and podcasts.

Additionally, Ms. Matthews has been sharing her prophetic life lessons as an Expert Author for EzineArticles.com. The demand for her prophetic discussions has also led to a new blog entitled, *Let's Talk Prophecy!*

More Titles
Available in Print and eBook formats

The War Journal (1999-2010) Volume I

Superheroes Of The Cross

END NOTES

[i] John 10:10

[ii] John 17:2-3

[iii] Ephesians 5:1

[iv] Genesis 37:3-11

[v] Genesis 11:1-9; 10:6-12; 9:8-19

[vi] Psalm 75:6-7

[vii] John 5:19; 12:49-50

[viii] Luke 11:14-20

[ix] Deuteronomy 4:23-31

[x] Galatians 3:28

[xi] Revelation 5:8-9

[xii] http://www.faith1publishing.com/shop-by-category/race-religion-and-racism.html

[xiii] Sid Roth, Interview with Chuck Pierce. Messianic Vision. 22. Aug. 2011. Radio <http://www.sidroth.org/site/News2?abbr=rad_&page=NewsArticle&id=10377&news_iv_ctrl=1121>

[xiv] Habakkuk 2:8

[xv] The Mayflower. Caleb Johnson's Mayflowerhistory.com. Web. 3 Mar. 2008. <http://www.mayflowerhistory.com/PrimarySources/MayflowerCompact.php>

[xvi] Deuteronomy 7:9; Psalm 105:8

[xvii] Galatians 6:7-8

[xviii] John 10:10

[xix] John 8:44

[xx] Matthew 11:12

[xxi] Matthew 23:1-5

[xxii] John 8:1-12

[xxiii] Jeremiah 1:4-5

[xxiv] Ephesians 1:1-14

[xxv] Jeremiah 29:11

[xxvi] Romans 11:1-36

[xxvii] Psalm 122:6

[xxviii] Genesis 16:1-6

[xxix] I Samuel 15:23; Hosea 4:6

[xxx] Ecclesiastes 12:13-14

[xxxi] Jeremiah 17:9-10

[xxxii] Genesis 8:20-22

[xxxiii] Romans 12:19

[xxxiv] Psalm 18:6-7; I Samuel 26:1-25

[xxxv] Genesis 18:16-33

[xxxvi] Job 42:7-17

[xxxvii] Acts 1:8

[xxxviii] I Corinthians 13:7
[xxxix] II Timothy 2:3, 10, 11-13

---

[i]*Waiting For Armageddon*. Dir(s) Davis; Sacchi, Heilbronner; 2009. Netflix Stream

www.ingramcontent.com/pod-product-compliance
Lightning Source LLC
Chambersburg PA
CBHW020750300326

41914CB00050B/49